Connected North

Illustrations copyright © 2021 by Nicole Josie.

All rights reserved. The use of any part of this publication reproduced, transmitted in any form or by any means, electronic, mechanical, photocopying, recording, or otherwise, or stored in a retrieval system, without the prior written consent of the publisher—or, in case of photocopying or other reprographic copying, a licence from the Canadian Copyright Licensing Agency—is an infringement of the copyright law.

Learning *with* Animals

by
Nicole Josie

**HATCHET LAKE FIRST NATION,
WOLLASTON LAKE, SASKATCHEWAN**

ËTTHËN HELDELI DENÉ
TRANSLATIONS BY FLORENCE ST. PIERRE

During a Connected North community visit to Hatchet Lake Denesuline First Nation in the community of Wollaston Lake several years ago, I had the opportunity to meet Dene artist Nicole Josie who shared her portfolio with me. We spoke about the importance of art as a way to support students with Dene language learning resources.

The breathtaking approach to the illustrations created for this Learning with Animals project truly amazed us all in the process and timeframe that they were developed. Together with Dene translations by Florence St. Pierre, we were delighted to assist with producing this incredible Learning with Animals Dene language resource!

The highlight in this process was hosting Nicole together with her family members in Saskatoon (Treaty 6 Territory) during the Spring of 2019 at an Art Gallery Exhibition featuring the works in this children's book. We are so grateful for the opportunity to collaborate with Father Megret Elementary School and others involved with Athabasca Denesuline Education Authority to support learning opportunities and resources for students!

We hope our work in co-developing resources like this one supports students in their own learning and connection to their communities, and contributes to language revitalization efforts.

Jennifer Corriero
Executive Director,
TakingITGlobal and Connected North

Nųltsį

SKUNK

1

Yáhtų́ę́

DEER

Thah

MARTIN

Tthejuze

MINK

4

ʔudaí

JACKFISH (PIKE)

Dzędhił

ELK

6

Ts'áili

FROG

7

Nąbie

OTTER

8

Gah

RABBIT

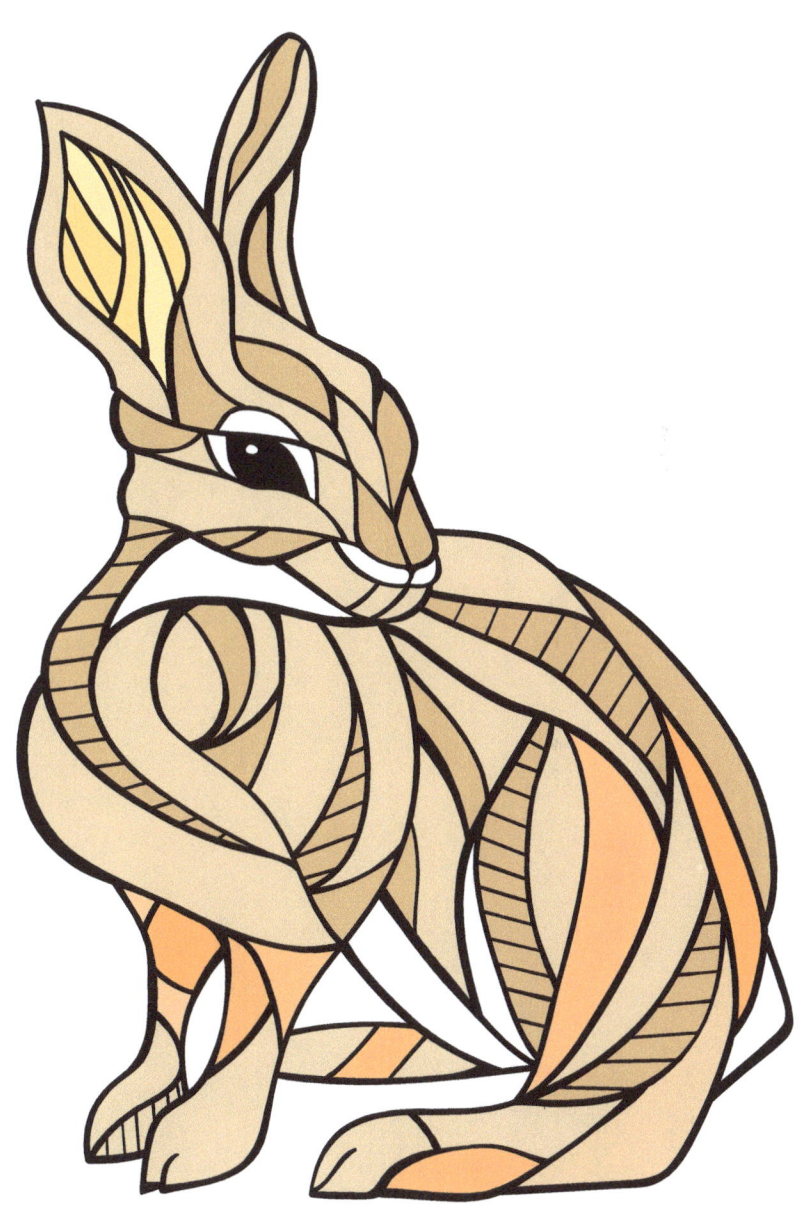

Mołdzaghe

OWL

10

Sas

BEAR

11

Nąghai

WOLVERINE

12

Deldele

SUCKER (FISH)

13

Tsá

BEAVER

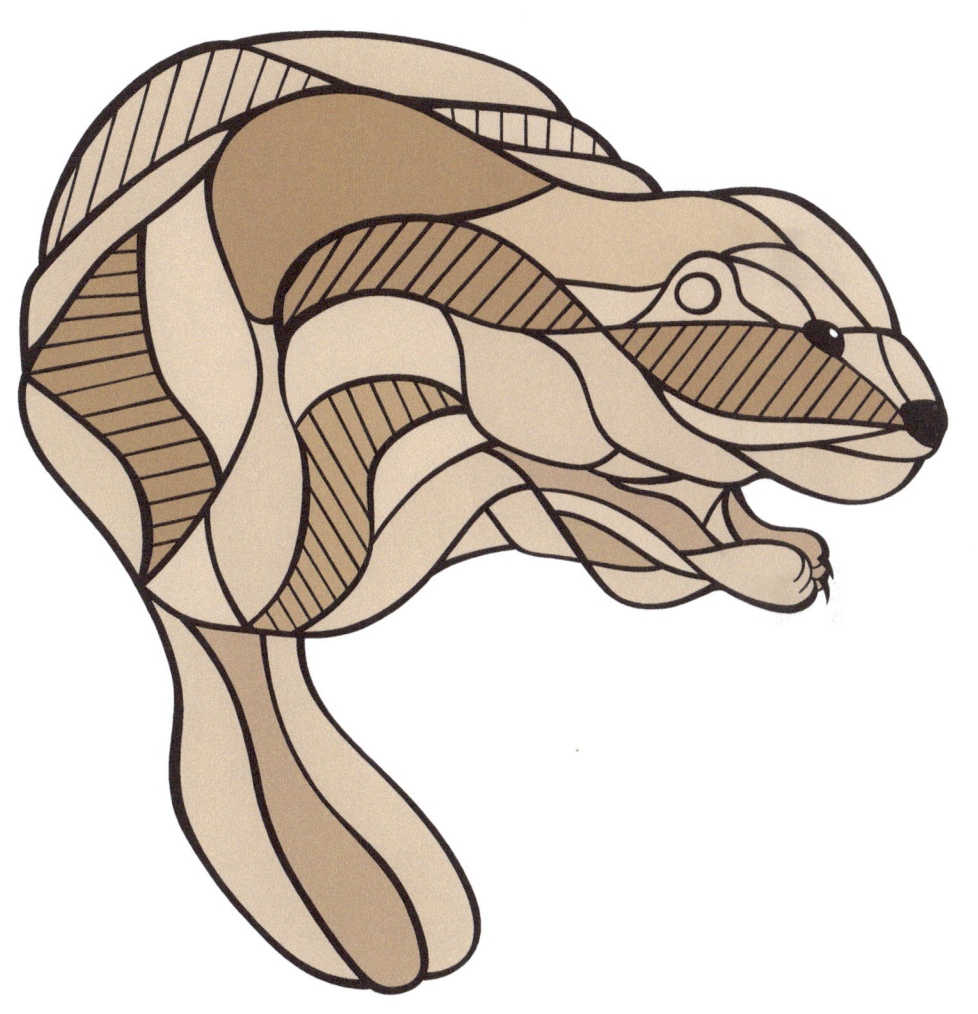

Łuezążę

TROUT

15

Jíze

BIRD (WHISKEYJACK)

Yágole

BUTTERFLY

17

K'áígúe

CATERPILLAR

18

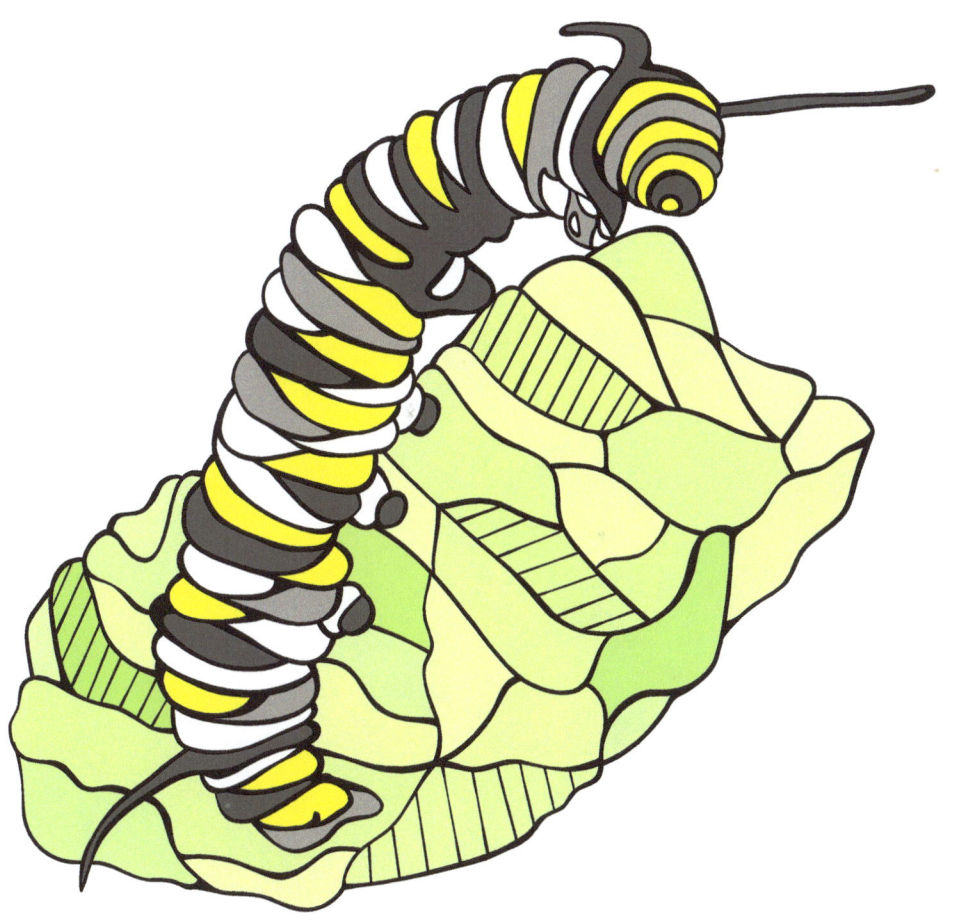

Nųnįe

WOLF

Diníe

MOOSE

Det'ani chogh

EAGLE

21

Dzɛn

MUSKRAT

Nągídhe

FOX

23

Chize

LYNX

24

Horádzie

SPIDER

25

Etthén

CARIBOU

26

Hhah

GOOSE

Łuh

WHITE (FISH)

28

Datsą tsele

RAVEN

Cheth

DUCK

30

Dlúne

MOUSE

31

Ts'i

PORCUPINE

32

Besk'áíyé

SEAGULL

33

Dadzęnę

LOON

34

Tł'izi tthoghé dheth

BEEHIVE

35

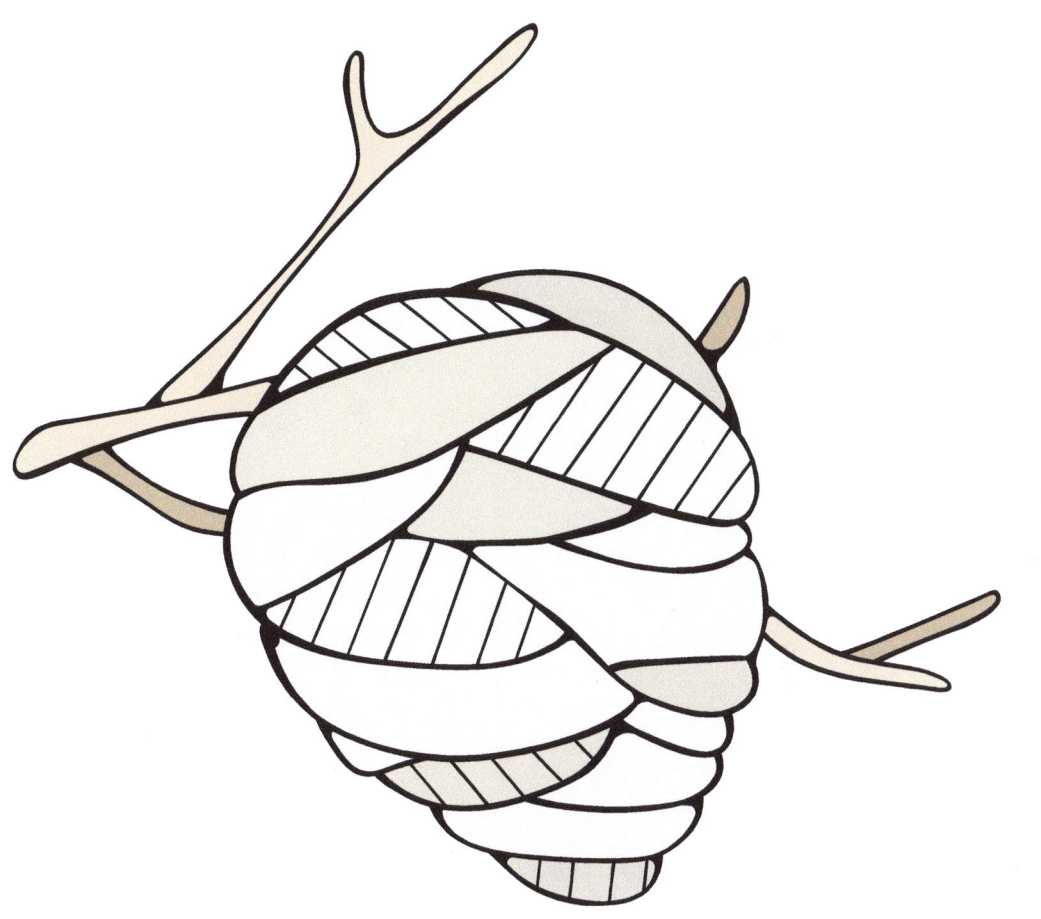

www.ingramcontent.com/pod-product-compliance
Lightning Source LLC
Chambersburg PA
CBHW041403090426
42743CB00006B/142